A souvenir guide

Knightshayes

Devon

D1470603

National Trust

A Complex Creation   2
4   The making of the Heathcoats
6   Builders and baronets
8   The commission
10 Burges' vision
12 Crace's revisions
14 The creation of the garden

Knightshayes in Layers   16
Burges
    17   on the outside
    18   in the Great Hall
    20   in the Burges Room
Burges meets Crace
    22   in the Billiard Room
    24   in the Library
Crace
    26   in the Dining Room
    28   in the Boudoir
    30   in the Bedroom Corridor
    32   in the Gentleman's Room
The Heathcoat Amorys
    34   in the Main Bedroom
    36   in the Smoking Room
    38   in the Morning Room
    40   in the Golf Room
All drawn together
    42   in the Drawing Room

The Making of a
Great Garden   44
45 The formal garden
48 The woodland garden
56 The working estate

At the Heart of Knightshayes   60
    Joining forces
    The outlook for Knightshayes

A Complex Creation

Knightshayes – an extraordinary 19th-century house and a great 20th-century garden – was created by the Heathcoat Amory family at the heart of the local community. It is a place of change, from the beginning and continuing to this very day.

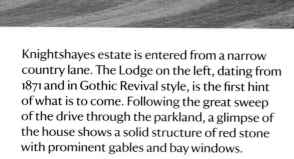

Knightshayes estate is entered from a narrow country lane. The Lodge on the left, dating from 1871 and in Gothic Revival style, is the first hint of what is to come. Following the great sweep of the drive through the parkland, a glimpse of the house shows a solid structure of red stone with prominent gables and bay windows.

An uncertain identity

In 1869 Sir John Heathcoat Amory commissioned the design of Knightshayes from one of the most extraordinary architects of the 19th century, William Burges. His designs were extravagant, lavish, hugely ambitious and all too much for the family.

Above **Knightshayes seen from the South Garden**

Whilst the exterior was largely completed to Burges' plans in 1874, another of the century's great designers, John Dibblee Crace, was brought in to tone down the scheme for the interiors.

Even these were considered too extravagant, and much of Burges' and Crace's work was covered up by successive generations of the family from the late 1880s right up until the 1960s. It seems that none of the Heathcoat Amorys ever fully took to living in the grand house, struggling to make it the warm and welcoming family home they wanted, and later generations turned their attentions instead to the garden.

Recognition at last

Knightshayes was left to the National Trust by Sir John Heathcoat Amory in 1972. Accepted initially for its outstanding 20th-century garden, the significance of the house was soon realised. Listed Grade I by English Heritage, its highest recognition of importance, the National Trust, with Lady Heathcoat Amory's support, began the long process of restoring the interiors of Knightshayes to their 19th-century designs. Today the house is in a delicate balance of restoration, reinstatement and recreation.

Above Flowering quince on the south front

Left Medieval yet playful – a tortoiseshell cat corbel in the Great Hall

The making of the Heathcoats

Knightshayes was the family home of the Heathcoat Amory family for 125 years, from 1872 to 1997. From a farming family in Derbyshire they grew, through their industry, to become the owners of the largest lace-making factory in the world. A family of philanthropists, they played a significant role at the heart of the community.

John Heathcoat (1783–1861)

Born near Derby in 1783 John Heathcoat was the son of a cattle farmer. Showing a propensity for hard work and inventiveness, he did several apprenticeships with makers of textile-weaving frames and, in 1805, completed the model of his first bobbin net machine. This machine transformed the lace-making industry from the slow, hand-made 'pillow and bobbin' method. Patented when John was only 25 years old, the design was to make him one of the great employers of the Midlands when he moved to Loughborough to start his factory.

Disaster strikes

His fortunes were about to change, however. On the night of 28 June 1816 Luddite wreckers, angry bands of English craftsmen afraid that this new invention might destroy the livelihood of traditional lace-makers, attacked the factory, demolishing the 55 lace frames with axe and hammer and setting fire to the lace. Within half an hour the building was a total loss and 200 men were out of work.

John refused £10,000 compensation to reinvest in his business in the Midlands. Characteristically stoical about the disaster, he moved instead to Tiverton, a town with a long tradition of woollen goods manufacture. Later that same year a disused textile mill was converted to create a large state-of-the-art factory, making fine lace net, mostly from silk. Together with many of his workers, who had followed him on foot to Tiverton knowing nothing of their destination but trusting entirely in their employer, John began manufacturing again and a hugely successful business resulted.

Self-made and much admired

In a speech at a public dinner in Tiverton in 1843 John Heathcoat recollected how he 'came almost like a ship-wrecked mariner cast away upon your shores'. The people of Tiverton did indeed prove to be his salvation, or at least certainly came to the rescue of his business, which was in real danger of foundering during the Luddite Rebellion. John repaid the loyalty of his workers, building houses, churches and schools for them, still distinguishable by their grey-painted doors.

From industry to local government, John became Member of Parliament for Tiverton in 1832. On his death in 1861 the sincere and spontaneous outpouring of grief from the town, with black cloth being laid for almost two miles all along the road from his home in Bolham to St Peter's Church, was testimony to a man who was much loved by all.

Above Luddite wreckers smashing lace frames

Right John Heathcoat's Tiverton Lace Manufactory, c.1836. All the royal wedding veils, from Queen Victoria to Princess Diana, have been made in Tiverton

Opposite John Heathcoat, the founder of the family fortunes; engraving by T. L. Atkinson after a portrait by William Beetham

Builders and baronets

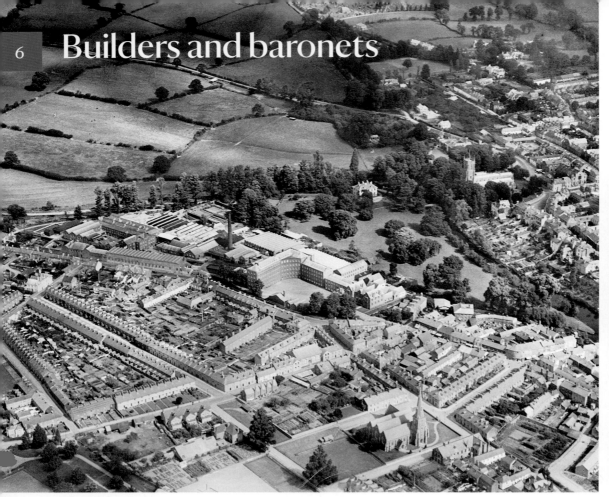

Sir John, 1st Bt (1829–1914)
The builder of Knightshayes

John Heathcoat had three daughters but his only son died in infancy and the business passed to his grandson, John. He was the first to take the name Heathcoat Amory, as his father Samuel Amory, John Heathcoat's business partner, had married John Heathcoat's daughter Anne. Born in 1829, John inherited the highly successful business when he was 32. However, John's passion was not for industry and, marrying Henrietta Unwin in 1863, he left the day-to-day running of the business to his brother-in-law, William Unwin.

His public duties, including Deputy Lieutenant of the county, Justice of the Peace and Liberal MP for Tiverton, led to him receiving a baronetcy in 1874 from the Prime Minister, William Gladstone, for 'political services'.

These duties, however, were not very demanding and left him plenty of time to indulge his sporting passions, shooting on his Scottish estate and fishing at his lodge in Norway. His great love was hunting across Exmoor with his three packs of hounds – staghounds, foxhounds and harriers. In 1868 John bought the Knightshayes estate. Little is

Above **Sir John Heathcoat Amory; by John Gray (Staircase)**

Above left **The factory and environs, 1928**

Opposite **Sir Ian Heathcoat Amory (1864–1931), 2nd Bt; by Frederic White (Drawing Room)**

known about the early history of the estate. The house that John found, standing about 100 metres from the present one, had been built in 1787 by merchant banker Benjamin Dickinson. This John demolished in order to build his new family home.

Sir Ian, 2nd Bt (1864–1931) The reformer

Sir John's eldest son, Sir Ian, and his brother Ludovic, took over the business on their father's death in 1914, on the eve of the First World War. Taking a much more active role in the business than Sir John, they strengthened the worker-owner relationship and introduced inspired reforms such as a pension scheme, one of the first in the country. Ludovic's tragic death aged 37, whilst serving with the Devon Yeomanry in France, was a profound loss for Sir Ian. The business suffered hard times during the trade depression of the 1920s but, with Sir Ian's two sons, John and Derick, now co-directors, the company expanded into producing new fabrics, such as crepes.

Sir John, 3rd Bt (1894–1972) The gardener and collector

On Sir Ian's death on 4 January 1931, following a hunting accident just before Christmas, his son John became the 3rd Baronet and owner of Knightshayes. With his brother Derick he continued technical developments at the factory. In 1936 he met Joyce Wethered, the celebrated lady golfer, at a golf match at Westward Ho! They were engaged within three months and married the following year. Together they followed their shared passions for developing the garden and collecting ceramics and fine paintings by Old Masters. On his death in 1972, Sir John gave Knightshayes, some of its contents and 262 acres of the estate to the National Trust, whilst his widow Joyce continued to live at the house, in the east wing, until her death in 1997.

Above The wedding of Sir John Heathcoat Amory and Joyce Wethered, 6 January 1937; by Bassano

Below Sir John Heathcoat Amory (1894–1972), 3rd Bt; by Mary Eastman

The commission

Knightshayes Court, built at the peak of Victorian country house building, was intended as a grand family home and a solid expression of Sir John's status and values. Sir John employed leading architect William Burges to draw up plans.

Previously known for his designs for church buildings, Burges was a brilliant and eccentric architect and a surprising choice for this Victorian industrialist. A copy of the great architect Pugin's *Contrasts*, a 14th-birthday present from his father, was the start of Burges' passion for Gothic architecture, which became a lifelong obsession. Medievalism ran through Burges' blood and, fuelled by his opium habit, his creative genius found full expression in his designs, both for exterior and interior schemes.

Burges travelled widely studying buildings. As Knightshayes shows, he developed his own unique style from the characteristics of early French and Italian Gothic but also with touches of Islamic inspiration and the strong chunky forms of High Victorian Gothic.

KINGS CROSS BATTLE BRIDGE
S George Arch'

CONTRASTED CROSSES

CHICHESTER CROSS

Opposite A watercolour by Burges of how he imagined Knightshayes in its garden setting, c.1868. The tower was never built

Opposite below William Burges, after Henry Van der Weyde

Above Pugin's *Contrasts* or *A Parallel Between the Noble Edifices of the Middle Ages, and Corresponding Buildings of the Present Day; Showing the Present Decay of Taste*

Right William Burges lived his medieval dreams

These medieval fantasy interiors were not to be realised. The exterior was built almost as he designed, with only two modifications – the reduction in height of the great tower over the staircase in the north-west corner and the changing of the axis of the Billiard Room to north–south. However, the lavish and expensive proposals for the interior were unacceptable to the family. Unlike Burges' work at Cardiff Castle and Castell Coch in the 1860s and 1870s, where he was able to fulfil his lavish schemes for the Marquis of Bute, his comparable vision for Knightshayes would remain only in his drawings.

'There's a babyish party named Burges,
Who from infancy scarcely emerges.
If you had not been told,
He's disgracefully old,
You would offer a bull's eye to Burges.'
Ditty by Dante Gabriel Rossetti

Nicknamed 'Billy' Burges, he was a prominent figure in the artistic avant-garde in London and friend of Gabriel Rossetti and other artists belonging to the Pre-Raphaelite Brotherhood. So deeply immersed in the Gothic was he that he had his own medieval outfit designed and his homes in London were a full-blooded expression of his dreams.

A touch too much

Whilst Burges' designs for the exterior were relatively restrained at Knightshayes, his formidable imagination created the most extraordinary and ambitious interior schemes. Presented to the Heathcoat Amorys in a lavish and beautifully illustrated 57-page folio album of watercolours in 1873, which remains at Knightshayes, the final scheme includes meticulous details from floors to ceilings, as well as furnishings.

Burges' vision

Burges' allegiance to the medieval was in everything he did. 'I was brought up in the 13th-century belief and in that belief I intend to die,' he proclaimed. His watercolours at Knightshayes show fantastic and richly designed interiors filled with sculpture, stained glass, mosaics, furniture and metalwork.

This page Burges' design for the Drawing Room, looking west

Inset Burges' design for the Drawing Room ceiling (see front cover)

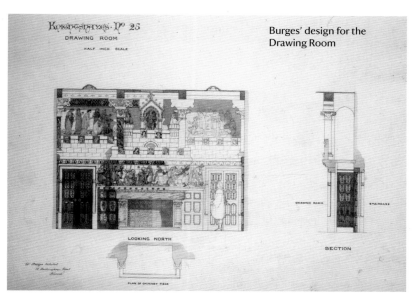

Burges' design for the Drawing Room

Left Burges' design for the Great Hall

Below left Burges' design for the Library

Below Burges' design for the Boudoir fireplace

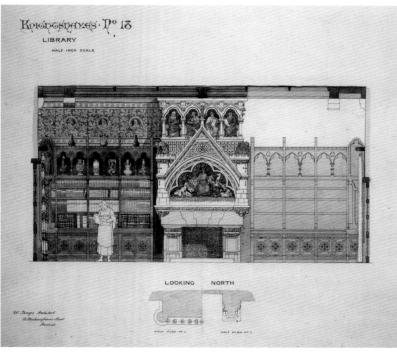

Crace's revisions

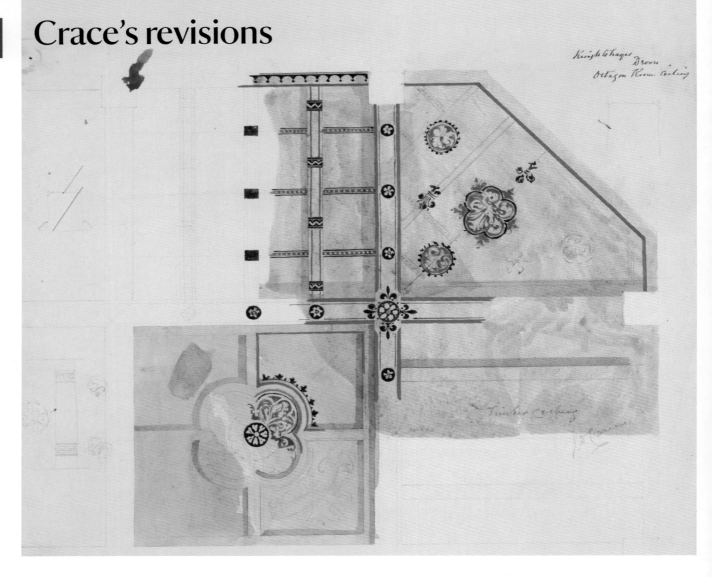

Knightshayes Devon
Octagon Room ceiling

In 1874 Burges was sacked and the family employed a less flamboyant designer to complete the interiors of Knightshayes, John Dibblee Crace (1838–1919). Coming from the highly prestigious family firm of interior decorators, which saw three generations of Craces working for royal and aristocratic clients, J. D. Crace was thought to be a far safer choice.

The external stonework at Knightshayes finished, Burges then moved on to the interior carvings, many of which were undertaken before Crace took over. Of Burges' designs only the structure and the stone- and wood-carvings were ever completed.

Surviving drawings, held in the Victoria and Albert Museum in London and dated between 1875 and 1882, illustrate the schemes created by

Above Crace's design for what was the Octagon Room, now the Morning Room

Opposite An early sketch by Crace of the roundels on the Boudoir ceiling

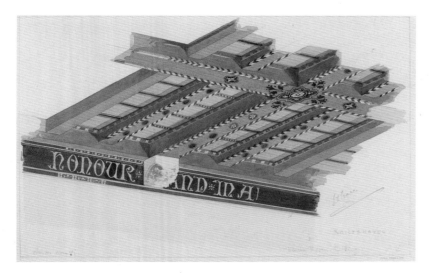

Above Crace's design for the Dining Room was largely realised

Above right Crace's design for the Gentleman's Room is comparable with today's restored scheme

Crace for the interiors. Governed to some extent by Burges' structure and designs, he created spaces of rich colour and delicately intricate detail, whilst toning down Burges' extravagance and drama. The result was far more in tune with his patrons' tastes and budget. His work was completed in 1883.

Yet, despite his toning down of Burges' designs, Crace's work, continuing in the Gothic Revival tradition, was still too elaborate for the family and even this was later covered over.

De-Gothicising Knightshayes

Despite all the attempts to satisfy the wishes of the family, further alteration of the vivid interiors was yet to come. In 1889, soon after Crace's work was completed, Sir John covered up his colourful Drawing Room ceiling (page 42). Many more changes were made in the 20th century. At a time when Victorian design was completely out of favour, many ornate ceilings, fireplaces and other features were covered up or removed to create interiors in a more or less Georgian style. Thankfully not much was actually destroyed.

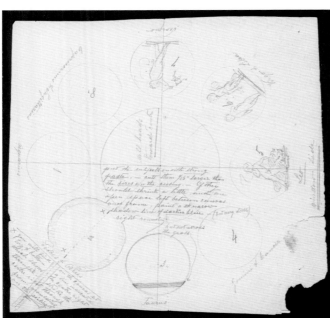

The Heathcoat Amorys were from early days unable to appreciate Victorian architecture.... Each generation has played its part in dismantling the most eccentric and ornate features in the house.'

Lady Heathcoat Amory, 1981

The creation of the garden

Above The head gardener between two gigantic topiary talbots (heraldic dogs)

The site on which Knightshayes was to be built was chosen for its elevated position and clear visual link with Tiverton and the factory. Following on from his choice of the most eminent architect of the day, Sir John engaged leading landscape gardener Edward Kemp (1817–91) for the garden.

Kemp originally created formal gardens close to the house, with terraces of bedding below the south front and a bowling green enclosed by yew hedges to the east. To the west he created the 'American Garden', a valley of ponds, waterfalls and rockeries planted with trees and shrubs, and planned the layout of the kitchen garden. However, like the house, the garden was transformed by successive generations.

A garden in decline

In the 1920s, under Sir Ian Heathcoat Amory's ownership, the Fox and Hounds topiary on top of the yew hedges was created but the rest of the garden was in decline. The Victorian scheme was out of fashion and too labour-intensive.

Described by Joyce, Lady Heathcoat Amory, the garden that greeted her arrival at Knightshayes in 1937 was 'confined to a few formal terraces, some bedding out, a tortuously clipped yew topiary and a small paved area with rose beds. The rest was given over to a bowling green and a large expanse of lawn.'

A new creative drive

Sir John and Lady Heathcoat Amory developed a passion for gardening and, after the Second World War, made its development a priority. As beginners, they sought advice from friends and acquaintances, including some of the great names in 20th-century gardening – the horticulturalists Graham Stuart Thomas OBE, Norman Hadden and deputy ranger of Windsor Great Park, Sir Eric Savill. It was Michael Hickson, head gardener from 1963 to 2003, who put much of this into practice.

An exceptional garden was created, at the heart of the parkland and estate, one of the finest in England with more than 1,200 species unique to Knightshayes. Recognised for their contributions to horticulture, Sir John, Lady Heathcoat Amory and Michael Hickson were each presented with the Victorian Medal of Honour, the Royal Horticultural Society's highest award.

Knightshayes is a designed landscape of outstanding national importance, recognised by English Heritage as Grade II* Registered status. It seems that the family had more success with, and more satisfaction from, the garden than the house.

Top Knightshayes boasts a four-acre Kitchen Garden and one of the most comprehensive plant collections in the care of the National Trust

Above Sir John (far left) and Lady Heathcoat Amory (second from right) with brother Roger and his wife on the Terraces

A garden with house attached

The importance of this 20th-century garden was the initial reason for the National Trust acquiring Knightshayes. Only later did the significance of the house become clear and the Trust's decision in the mid-1970s to restore the interiors to their Victorian peak was an ambitious one. Much of the contents owned by the family had left the house and so rooms have been refurnished with gifts, purchases and loans. Slowly, room by room, and with Lady Heathcoat Amory's full support, the restoration has been achieved.

'Look here, if we get through this [the War] all right, we'll make a garden together.'

Sir John to Joyce

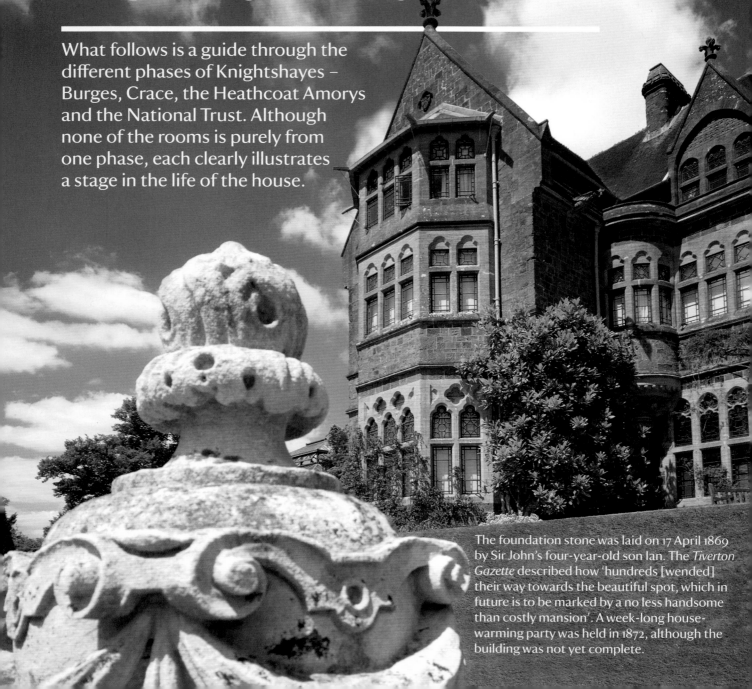

Knightshayes in Layers

What follows is a guide through the different phases of Knightshayes – Burges, Crace, the Heathcoat Amorys and the National Trust. Although none of the rooms is purely from one phase, each clearly illustrates a stage in the life of the house.

The foundation stone was laid on 17 April 1869 by Sir John's four-year-old son Ian. The *Tiverton Gazette* described how 'hundreds [wended] their way towards the beautiful spot, which in future is to be marked by a no less handsome than costly mansion'. A week-long house-warming party was held in 1872, although the building was not yet complete.

Burges
on the outside

Knightshayes was described in the *Building News* **in 1870 as 'stately and bold and its medievalism is not obtrusive'. Burges' design for the exterior of Knightshayes would have been admired by Victorian connoisseurs of architecture for its 'muscular' Gothic elevations, unmoulded mullions and simple but varied plate tracery.**

The entrance front
The impressive façade is of red Hensley stone with Ham stone dressings. The exterior is deliberately asymmetrical and reflects the layout inside – notably the Great Hall's own separate roof and large windows, and the great staircase tower. A stone talbot (a hunting dog featured on the family's coat of arms) sits high up on a small belfry and gargoyles project from the roofline. The Billiard Room on the left screens the servants' courtyard.

Left This feature is known as plate tracery because the glazed openings appear to be cut out of a flat plate of masonry

The Tiverton front
The façade facing the town is more subtly asymmetrical, although Burges' hand can be seen in the steep roofs, the continuation of massive carved gargoyles and an angel in the central gable. The east wing contains the Burges-designed kitchen, facing north into a courtyard, and a serving room and butler's pantry, facing the garden. It is modestly subservient to the house itself and balanced by the 1963 addition of the Conservatory to the west.

The Porch and Screens Passage
The house is entered through the Porch, passing beneath a carved stone medieval figure by Thomas Nicholls, which acts as a lantern-bearer over the door. As in any great medieval house, the Great Hall is preceded by a screens passage. The screen, having been removed by the family in about 1914, was restored by the National Trust in the 1990s to the original Burges design, thanks in part to some timber fragments found in the basement.

Above A fierce gargoyle on the entrance front

Opposite An ornamental urn on the terrace below the south front

Below A medieval lantern-bearer over the entrance

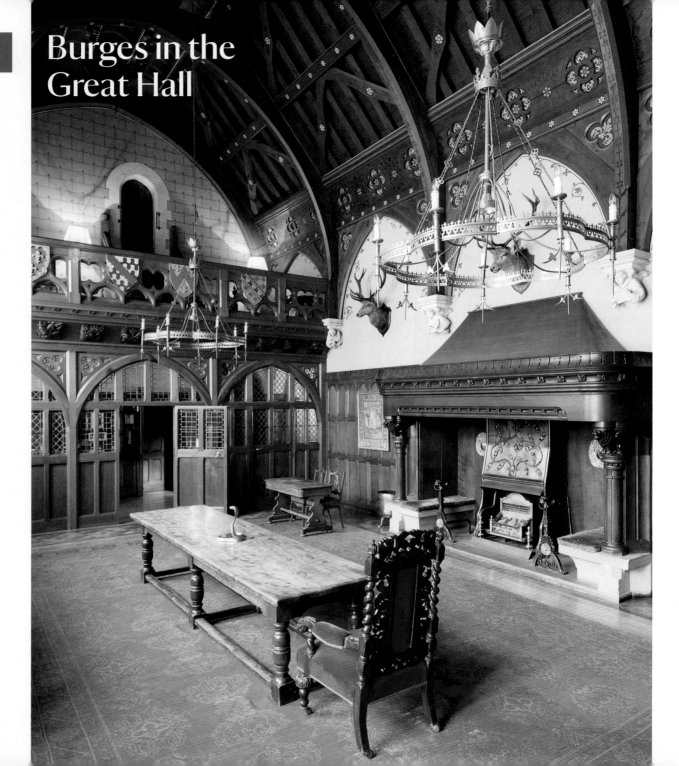

Burges in the Great Hall

Opposite The Great Hall looking towards the Screens Passage and Gallery

Right Burges' design for the Great Hall fireplace

Below left A stone corbel of a harvester with a sickle and sheaves of corn, to the left of the fireplace

Below right A cowled woman with yarn

Inspired by medieval halls, the room soars to the roof trusses, which spring from corbels 'representing the conditions of Life'. The walls and roof were to be elaborately stencilled and the whole room lit by stained-glass windows, whilst the chimneypiece was to rise to the roof.

A single surviving old photograph of the Great Hall taken *c*.1911, just before the family altered the room, shows that the main architectural features were built but the stencilled decoration was undertaken in a simpler design by Crace.

In addition to demolishing the screen, the family had the fireplace hood reduced in size and the stencilling erased in 1914. In the 1990s, using the original Burges designs and traces of coloured paintwork, the National Trust was able to reinstate the stencilling of the roof and restore the wall decoration and Turkish screen on the landing overlooking the Great Hall.

The huge teak staircase is also by Burges but newel posts carved with talbots were substituted for his planned carvings of St George and the dragon. The pairs of doors opposite the stairs formerly led to the Drawing Room but were later blocked.

Contents of note

The sketch by Burges shows the original design for the Hall's fireplace, and the painting by Axel Haig (1835–1921) of the Winter Smoking Room at Cardiff Castle in 1870 by Burges illustrates how similar the interiors at Knightshayes would have looked, had his full extravagant scheme gone ahead.

The huge Melbury Road Bookcase was designed by Burges and painted by many of his artist friends from the Pre-Raphaelite Brotherhood, including Edward Burne-Jones and Dante Gabriel Rossetti. Made in 1859–62 to house Burges' books on art in his own London homes, the bookcase is displayed here thanks to the generous loan by the Ashmolean Museum in Oxford.

The needlework is by Herbert Newton Wethered, father of Joyce, Lady Heathcoat Amory, and the stag heads are trophies from the first Baronet's hunting expeditions.

Burges in the Burges Room

Opposite The Burges Room

Right The wall decoration in the Burges Room features 87 species of bird and one monkey

In Burges' words, 'the great feature of [the] medieval chamber is the furniture; this in a rich apartment would be covered with paintings, both ornaments and subjects; it not only did its duty as furniture, but spoke and told a story'. But, like his other medieval-style interiors, the vision was never realised.

The great album of watercolours presented to the Heathcoat Amorys by Burges in 1873 included a typically ambitious design for this bedroom. From the painted ceiling to the stencilled walls and decorated fireplace, the room was to be a riot of colour and delicate detail, with only the walls below the dado rail being painted a single plain colour, perhaps as a foil for the elaborately painted furniture with which Burges intended to furnish the room.

Re-envisaging the scene

When the National Trust acquired Knightshayes, the room was painted in a neutral cream colour and, apart from a fireplace, it had no architectural features whatsoever.

In 2001 it was decided to arrange and decorate the room as Burges had intended.

The upper walls are painted with birds perched on stylised branches and identified in Gothic script, a similar theme to that used by Burges in his Buckingham Street house in London. In total 87 native and exotic species of birds and one monkey are depicted, each different – with the exception of two geese and two magpies. These have been faithfully reproduced from Burges' design for the room.

The fireplace is enclosed beneath a painted hood and the ceiling decorated with an enriched geometric pattern.

The room was opened by Jimmy Page, the lead guitarist of Led Zeppelin, on 28 May 2002. A passionate collector of Victorian Gothic furniture, Jimmy lives in Tower House in Kensington, Burges' former home.

Contents of note

The items in this room are mostly on loan from the Victoria and Albert Museum in London.

The Golden Bed was designed in 1879 for the guest bedroom in Burges' home at Tower House in London.

The pair of painted cabinets, also designed by Burges, was commissioned by a great patron of his, Herbert Yatman, in 1858.

Burges meets Crace in the Billiard Room

Every well-appointed Victorian country house had a billiard room, usually with its own WC and washroom. Burges' initial idea was a bow-fronted room parallel with the house but he eventually designed the present room, with top lighting from a large skylight, subsequently covered over.

Having served as a restaurant for visitors until 1988, the National Trust reinstated the decorative scheme of this room. Burges' design for the interior included a painted and gilded ceiling, 'with the addition of small silvered glasses' to represent stars on a red and blue ground. The present ceiling, however, was reinstated following Crace's scheme, the one originally undertaken for the

Below Stone corbels representing three of the Seven Deadly Sins

Heathcoat Amorys. Burges' walls were to have 'red lines on white ground with medallions containing figures of virtues and various animals representing the vices' above polished mahogany panelling.

It seems that the figures of the Virtues were never completed but the Vices are represented on the carved stone corbels by the Seven Deadly Sins. The owl, depicted on the eighth corbel, represents Wisdom. A marble fireplace with a gilded and mirrored overmantel was to have completed the Burges scheme but was never built, the present one being by Crace.

Contents of note

The billiard table, built by Thurston's of London, is original to the house.

The large sideboard is one of the few pieces of furniture in the house actually designed by Burges. Originally made for Worcester College, Oxford, where Burges redesigned the interior of James Wyatt's Neo-classical dining hall in 1874–79, it has been generously loaned by the College to Knightshayes since 1975.

The inscribed silver tray was a gift to Sir John from his factory employees on his marriage to Joyce Wethered in 1937.

Above **Burges' corbels meet Crace's ceiling in the Billiard Room**

Burges meets Crace in the Library

Burges let his creativity loose in his designs for the Library: Gothic bookcases nearly 10-feet high with niches for pottery; an embossed leather frieze, gilded and painted with portraits of classical authors; a castellated, painted and gilded chimneypiece. In the end only the jelly-mould ceiling, one of Burges' favourite features, was built.

Crace tempered this design with his own version in 1879. A drawing by him, now at the Victoria and Albert Museum, shows the Gothic bookcases of a similar height to that intended by Burges but with the cupboard doors plainly decorated with linenfold panelling. The decorative frieze above them was simply embossed leather. Two photographs of the room, from about 1900, indicate that it was built virtually as Crace had planned, including Burges' carved corbels and jelly-mould vaults, inspired by Arabic architecture.

20th-century alterations

In the 1950s the family lowered and narrowed the bookcases to a third of their original height and width, and removed their Gothic details. The chimneypiece was replaced with a new one, in the 18th-century style, and the ceiling covered in order to simplify the decorative scheme.

In 1984, the National Trust began restoring the room to Crace's designs. The removal of the false ceiling revealed Burges' elaborate decoration and jelly moulds. The lincrusta (a deeply embossed wall covering which was painted and gilded to resemble leather) was completed in the winter of 1998. Crace's fireplace and a few fragments of the shelves were found in store so that, with the evidence of drawings and photographs, a complete restoration of the walnut fittings was eventually possible in 1998.

The final task of filling the 160 feet of shelves required an appeal to National Trust members

Far left A photograph from *c.*1900 shows Crace's version of Burges' design

Left A later photograph, *c.*1970, shows the Library's simplified decoration and Burges' jelly-mould ceiling covered up

Above Burges' design for a
medieval library with
Gothic bookcases

Above right The Library
restored to Crace's design
and with Burges' ceiling
uncovered

to add to the few books originally belonging to
the family, the nucleus of whose collection had
been formed by Samuel Amory, the 1st
Baronet's father, in the early 19th century.

Contents of note

The old photographs illustrate the Library in
use as a sitting room and have been used by
the National Trust to furnish the room. The
three family portraits of John Heathcoat,
Samuel Amory and Ludovic Heathcoat Amory
are all by unknown English artists.

The Boulle bracket clock was a present
given to Sir Ian when he retired as Master of
the Tiverton Staghounds, a hunt he had
founded in 1896.

Crace in the Dining Room

the frieze and wall decorations, using lincrusta paper to imitate plaster. In the 1950s the room was again changed when a kitchen was installed and the room partitioned so that Sir John could incorporate a workshop in the window.

Writing on the wall

Using paint traces and Crace's drawings the National Trust was able to reinstate Crace's scheme for the ceiling. The lincrusta paper removed, Crace's frieze and inscriptions from two poems by Robert Burns were discovered, along with a line from Chaucer's *Manciple's Tale of Phoebus and the Crow*, almost complete: 'BE BLEST WITH HEALTH AND PEACE AND SWEET CONTENT; KEEP THY TONGUE AND KEEP THY FRIENDS; COME EASE, COME TRAVIL, COME PLEASUR, COME PAIN, MY WARST WORD IS WELCOME AND WELCOME AGAIN'.

The National Trust was unable to rescue Crace's wallpaper so a new paper, copied from a Crace design used in the House of Lords, was hung in its place.

For this room Burges proposed walls panelled in walnut and above this a carved inscription, the ceiling to be coloured and gilded, and stained-glass windows illustrating the fables of Aesop. As an additional luxury the room would have not one but two painted and gilded chimneypieces with canopies studded with armorial devices.

Of this scheme it seems that nothing was executed save the carving on the doors and a reduced version of the panelling, and so the room today is a restoration of Crace's design. Crace's drawings of the ceiling are in the Victoria and Albert Museum and show that he adapted Burges' designs, including the sculptures of birds, animals and faces in the corbels, but the ceiling had been covered by the family at the end of the 19th century, as had

Happy memories

Memories of the room include those of a guest of the family in the early 20th century, a Miss March Phillips:

'On a hunting day it was such fun staying at Knightshayes – the sideboard loaded with cold ham, galantine and other meats, sliced bread and a pile of greaseproof paper and you just went and made your own sandwiches and took as much as ever you wanted.'

Sir John, 3rd Baronet remembered how lunchtimes were time for planning entertainments for all: his grandmother, Henrietta, would offer hunting, driving or shooting in the winter and cricket or croquet in the summer. For more formal parties, the large dining table would have been laid with the family silver, brought up from the safe in the basement. Up to 30 people could be seated and waited on by the butler and footmen.

Crace in the Boudoir

Right Burges' design for the Boudoir ceiling

Below left Crace's Zodiac roundels on the Boudoir ceiling

Below The Boudoir

The Boudoir was the private sitting room for the lady of the house. Burges was to have none of his decorative schemes realised. In one of these the lower walls were to be painted to simulate fabric with a frieze illustrating scenes from Tennyson's *Dream of Fair Women* **and a border of colourful birds.**

Stained glass was to fill every window and the ceiling would have sparkled with little circular mirrors amongst low-relief medallions painted with subjects from Tennyson and Chaucer. The chimneypiece was to show a swimming mermaid supporting a shelf with art pottery. This design, however, did not go to waste and Burges installed a similar chimneypiece in his own home, Tower House in Kensington.

A celestial ceiling

The less extravagant designs by Crace, with a more sober treatment of cedar panelling and a stone fireplace with carved timber surround, were implemented. The ceiling, however, was more ornately treated by Crace with a series of eight roundels each painted with signs of the Zodiac, several of which illustrated two signs combined within one painting. Not long after completion they were obliterated. Although Crace's original drawings were not detailed enough to allow an accurate restoration, the National Trust commissioned the repainting of the roundels by Ian Cairnie in 1981, closely following a similar scheme devised by Crace which survives in a house in Hill Street, London. In 1991 the room was hung with wallpaper copied from a design by Burges, now at the Royal Institute of British Architects in London.

Below left **Mary Cawthorne, Mrs Morley Unwin; by Arthur Devis**

Below right **Alexandra Seymour, Lady Heathcoat Amory; by Frank Copnall**

Family portraits

The portrait of Alexandra Seymour, Lady Heathcoat Amory, by Frank Copnall (1870–1949) is one of the key items in the Boudoir. Wife of Sir Ian, the 2nd Baronet and mother of Sir John, who gave Knightshayes to the National Trust, she is depicted reading a letter, said to be sent by her son from school.

Also important is the earliest family portrait in the house, of Mary Cawthorne, Mrs Morley Unwin, the great-great-grandmother of the first Sir John's wife and close friend of the poet William Cowper, painted by Arthur Devis (1711/12–87).

The third family portrait in the Boudoir is the miniature of Sir John Heathcoat Amory, 3rd Baronet as a child of four painted by Lucas Henrey in 1898. Lastly, although not a family portrait, the 18th-century portrait of a *Girl in A Red Dress* is interesting. Painted on glass, it is indigenous to the house, collected by the family, rather than brought in by the National Trust to furnish the room.

Crace in the Bedroom Corridor

This space, linking the rooms along the first floor of the house, was originally stencilled following Crace's design. However this was covered over by the family. In 1976 the National Trust investigated the walls of the corridor to find, firstly, a late 19th-century wallpaper and, underneath that, Crace's original pattern.

The re-instatement of this stencilled decoration was undertaken by the London firm of decorators which had undertaken the original

A convenient solution

The water closet was cleverly incorporated into a small room off the Bedroom Corridor and decorated with a Burges-style wallpaper hung in 1991. This was the answer to the Victorians' problem, described by a writer on country house planning, as the 'difficulty to select positions for convenience which shall at the same time be suitable for privacy. The principles of English delicacy are not easily satisfied'.

work, Campbell Smith & Co. Established in 1873, the firm is still in existence today.

The *Portrait of a Gentleman* at the end of the corridor is of the works manager at the Heathcoat factory, Harry Salmon.

The oak buffet was designed in about 1860 by another Gothic Revival architect William White (1825–1900) for a nearby Victorian country house, Bishops Court near Exeter. It was bought by the National Trust in 1994.

Left *Portrait of a Gentleman*, or Harry Salmon, painted by Frederic Willie

Opposite The Bedroom Corridor

Crace in the Gentleman's Room

This room was originally called 'the Gentleman's Room' in Burges' plans for the house and the 'Small Library' in the 1899 inventory. Serving as a private retreat in the male domain, the gentleman's counterpart to the lady's Boudoir, it may well have been used as a smoking room until the new one was built in 1901.

Probably also used for estate business, the room had access from the east wing – a tenant passing through the main house was to be avoided at all costs. Subsequently it became known as the Gun Room but all the fittings and the fireplace were later removed. In 1989 it was converted to an exhibition room but today is shown once more as a gentleman's room.

Below The original plaster decoration in the adjoining lavatory

Right The Gentleman's Room from where estate affairs were managed

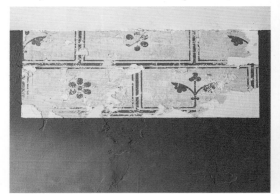

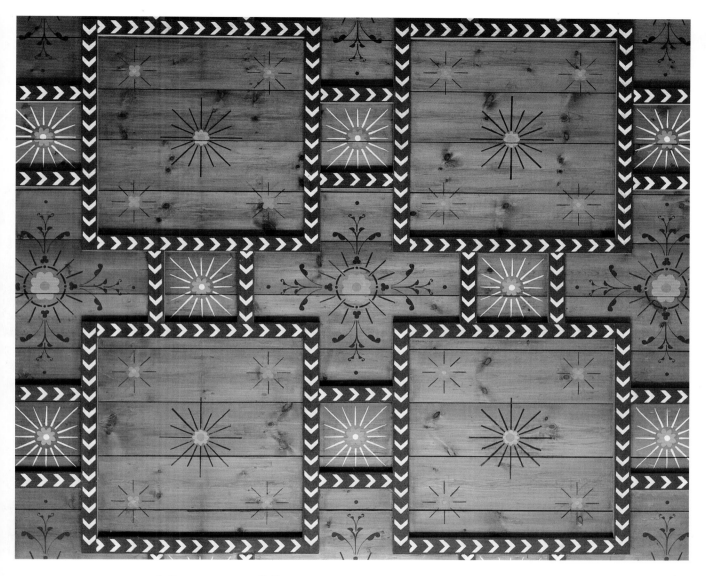

Above Crace's ceiling in the Gentleman's Room

A fragment of Crace

The decorative scheme of the room, elaborately designed by Burges to include a ceiling painted with the sun surrounded by signs of the Zodiac, figures in niches 'showing the occupations of the year' on the walls and a chimneypiece incorporating a stag hunt with hounds leaping out of the canopy, was never undertaken. Even Crace's more moderate scheme was removed in the early 20th century but has now been restored by the National Trust. The ceiling has been repainted and the walls covered in wallpaper, reproduced from a fragment of the original found in the adjoining lavatory where it can still be seen, and, unusually, hung horizontally. Only the picture rails remain of Burges' scheme.

The Heathcoat Amorys in the Main Bedroom

Burges' original watercolour illustrating his intended scheme for this room shows the lower half of the walls painted yellow ochre with the frieze on the upper half depicting birds amidst a red leaf pattern. Unlike other rooms at Knightshayes, no Crace designs for this room survive, so were possibly never produced.

Below The bedcover was stitched by guests of Alexandra, wife of Sir Ian, 2nd Baronet

Family furniture and lace

The large pieces of furniture in the Main Bedroom – the late 18th-century English mahogany four-poster bed and Dutch wardrobe and corner cupboard of a similar date – were owned by the family. The display of wedding garments includes a dress, veil and gloves. The factory, now called Heathcoat Fabrics and no longer owned by the family, has produced all the royal wedding veils from Queen Victoria to Princess Diana, and continues the tradition of giving female employees a veil to wear on their wedding day.

The curved passage between the Main Bedroom and the Boudoir was originally a private alcove, accessible only from the Boudoir. The National Trust created the opening, to allow access directly between the two rooms.

In 1973 the family moved a marble fireplace from the bedroom to the east wing of the house. A new carved oak surround was installed by the National Trust, who also laid the carpet and hung the wallpaper, both made in 1979. The room has a superb view over the parkland and a distant, but intentionally key, view of the Heathcoat factory in Tiverton.

Above The oriel window in the passage between the Main Bedroom and Boudoir

Right *Moonbeams Dipping into the Sea*, by Pre-Raphaelite painter Evelyn de Morgan (1855–1919)

The Heathcoat Amorys in the Smoking Room

Sir John used the small Gentleman's Room adjacent to the Billiard Room until in 1901 he employed Ernest George & Yates, the architectural firm, to design 'an apartment specially dedicated to the use of tobacco', with WC and lavatory (at the time 'lavatory' meant a place for washing).

A smoking room was part of the male domain in many Victorian country houses. It is possible that Burges intended to create a lavish room in the great tower at the north-east corner of the house, which was never built, as he had at Cardiff Castle for Lord Bute, where tower rooms were designated as summer and winter smoking rooms.

Above The Winter Smoking Room at Cardiff Castle

Opposite The Smoking Room

A room of many uses

The male members of the family and guests would have retired to the Smoking Room after dinner in the evening, whilst it was used by younger members of the family during the day. Teas were sometimes served here, when the garden was open to the public, or for meetings of the Tiverton Girl Guides, of whom Joyce, Lady Heathcoat Amory was a great supporter and for whom she was a Divisional Commissioner for 12 years.

The Heathcoat Amorys' philanthropy manifested itself in many ways, including the purchase of a mansion in Tiverton for the town's Aged People Association and provision of a site for the Red Cross's headquarters.

Learn about the family

The room remains as it has always been, except for a new door created by the National Trust through to the entrance front. Originally used by the Trust as a reception and shop, it was furnished in 1988 as an Edwardian smoking room. Family memorabilia and photographs on display reveal more about the history of Knightshayes.

A two-thirds size facsimile of Burges' original album of watercolours (presented to Sir John in 1873) is laid out on the table, showing his interior schemes for eight rooms on the ground floor and three on the first floor. The bust of Sir John, 3rd Baronet is by Sir Jacob Epstein.

Household staff
The family employed a large staff to run the house and estate. In the early 20th century, when Sir Ian and Alexandra, Lady Heathcoat Amory lived at Knightshayes, the indoor staff consisted of the butler (Mr Elton), two footmen, three housemaids, a personal maid (Mr Elton's wife) for Lady Alexandra, the cook (Mrs Babbage), a kitchen maid, a scullery maid, an odd-job man and an electrician. The latter, Mrs Babbage's husband, was required to manage the electricity at the house, generated by water turbines on the River Exe a mile away. Sir Ian also employed a secretary, Miss Coles.

The Heathcoat Amorys in the Morning Room

The Morning Room, called 'the Octagon Room' in the 1899 inventory, faces south and was used as a daytime sitting room. The room says much about the interests of Sir John and Joyce, Lady Heathcoat Amory, and was where they displayed their collection of Old Masters, some of which are still on view today.

Burges' decorative scheme showed a vivid combination of colours, textures and materials: partially ebonised panelled walls beneath a frieze of grisaille figures; stained glass; a panelled and decorated ceiling; a Gothic chimneypiece in red 'Emperor Marble'; and, in the four corners, gilded niches supported by brass columns.

Above A copy of a self-portrait after Rembrandt

Above right *A Lady in a White Cap* in the manner of Holbein

Right *Madonna and Child with St Jerome and St Sebastian*; by Matteo di Giovanni

fortunately before prices increased astronomically. The pictures finally chosen were widely selected…. This is a collection in which each picture had a special meaning for us.'

Paintings and pots

Sir John and Lady Heathcoat Amory's passion for collecting ceramics resulted in the remarkable collection of 17th-century Italian maiolica (tin-glazed earthenware), which includes a pair of large drug jars. The paintings in this room, including a self-portrait after Rembrandt, a lady in a white cap in the manner of Holbein and, oldest of all, the *Madonna and Child with St Jerome and St Sebastian* by Matteo di Giovanni, are the remains of the original collection, the others having been bequeathed to museums. Following study, all but four have been found not to have been painted by the artists whose names appear on the frames.

Crace's design for the ceiling decoration, shown in a watercolour of 1874, was carried out but covered up in the 20th century. In the 1950s the family used the room as a dining room, with French windows installed to give access to the garden, and simplified the decorative scheme with white walls and a false ceiling.

In 1975 the National Trust began to restore the room, revealing Crace's original compartmented ceiling and repainting it with a new centrepiece and motto. Based on the 1899 inventory of the room and the discovery of red fabric threads in a window bay, the walls were later re-hung with red velvet. The chimneypiece and carpet, woven to incorporate the family's crest, were also installed.

A shared passion

Writing in 1981 about their destruction of Victoriana between 1950 and 1970, Lady Heathcoat Amory said that the Morning Room was to provide 'a suitable background for a small but very fine collection of Old Masters. It was understood that any purchase had to be approved together, which made it such an absorbing interest for both of us. We began soon after the War in a very modest way, the collection growing over the next 20 years,

The Heathcoat Amorys in the Golf Room

This was a waiting room where those with business to discuss would have sat before being admitted to the Gentleman's Room. It is not known if Burges ever designed a scheme for this room. The National Trust converted the room in 1989 to house an exhibition about Lady Heathcoat Amory's hugely successful golfing career.

Above American golfer Bobby Jones described Joyce's swing as the best he had ever seen

'I have never played with any golfer, man or woman, amateur or professional, who made me feel so utterly outclassed.'

Bobby Jones, American golfer, about Joyce

Left The Joyce Wethered Trophy by Anne Richardson

From her first experience of golf on a course laid out for children whilst on a family holiday in north Cornwall, and with only a very occasional lesson thereafter, Joyce became the English Ladies' Champion at the age of 19 and retained the title for the next four seasons. In addition, she won the British Ladies' Open Golf Championship four times in the 1920s and was considered to be the finest lady golfer of her generation, if not of the 20th century. The golf writer Herbert Warren Wind said that Joyce had 'the most correct and most lovely swing golf has ever known'.

Joyce also managed the golf department of Fortnum & Masons in the 1930s. Sir John like his wife was a keen and accomplished golf player, as well as being president and one of the founding members of the Tiverton Golf Club in 1932. When Sir John played, his butler often used to caddy for him – a fine sight in formal dark suit and black bowler hat!

A remarkable career

Lady Heathcoat Amory was much involved in the arrangement of the displays and the exhibition was opened by her and Peter Alliss, the professional golfer. The watercolour of Joyce was painted by her father, Herbert Newton Wethered. The glass cabinet displays some of her many medals and a large silver cup, made by one of the foremost English silversmiths, Omar Ramsden, using silver melted down from her trophies – Lady Heathcoat Amory's solution to the problem of where to put her many cups.

The blazer was awarded to her in 1975, on her election to the American World Golf Hall of Fame. The bronze Joyce Wethered Trophy, much prized by her, depicts a lady golfer of the 1920s and is the original of a trophy awarded annually to young female golfers.

Above The cup made by Omar Ramsden to celebrate Joyce's many golfing victories

The displays also include scrapbooks containing newspaper cuttings of her career, photographs and a copy of *Golf From Two Sides*, written in 1923 by Joyce and her brother Roger, also a well-known golfer. An old golf bag containing hickory-shafted golf clubs, with names like 'mashie' and 'niblick', dates from the early 20th century.

Above Joyce painted by her father, Herbert Newton Wethered

Left Joyce leading spectators and players during her win in the final of the Ladies' British Open Amateur Championship at St Andrews, Scotland, on 18 May 1929

All drawn together in the Drawing Room

The Drawing Room demonstrates a mixture of sources – the bones of Burges' design, Crace's ceiling and the National Trust's reinstatements of earlier decorations. Important family paintings and furnishings acquired by the Trust bring the room together.

Drawing on Burges

Burges' design for this room, where the ladies entertained and the annual servants' balls were held, would have been the climax of his interior schemes. Basing his theme on chivalry, Burges designed the chimneypiece to resemble a medieval castle, with a columned gallery above the fireplace, accessible from a secret spiral staircase, where ladies could look upon the gentlemen below. Painted wall panelling, a richly decorated frieze, stained glass, a star-spangled ceiling and a second great chimneypiece were also part of Burges' proposal.

Drawing on Crace

Only the staircase and Crace's toned-downed version of the ceiling, his chimneypiece on the end wall and the double doors on either side leading to the main staircase and Great Hall were ever built. Even these elements did not last for long, with the ceiling being covered in plaster panels in 1889.

Crace's chimneypiece on the north wall was removed in 1946 by the family and replaced with one in an 18th-century style on the long wall to the Library. The doorways were converted to display cabinets and, in 1963, the west bay was greatly enlarged by removing the central marble column of the twin arches, and installing French windows to the new conservatory. Sir John and Lady Joyce Heathcoat Amory furnished the room with Georgian pieces, comfortable armchairs and sofas and Old Master paintings.

Recent restorations

The National Trust discovered a brightly coloured design featuring Burges' gilded jelly-moulds behind the false ceiling's plaster panels. At the same time, in 1980, traces of coloured stencilling were found underneath layers of cream paint on the window mullions. Restoration was carried out in 1981, when the present marble chimneypiece, of the same scale as that originally planned for the room, was installed. Designed in 1876 by Burges for the hall at Worcester College, Oxford, it was removed from there in 1966 and later generously given to the Trust.

Finally, in 1982, the Trust restored the west bay column and arches, using timber painted to match the stone originals. The doors to the Hall currently remain blocked.

Contents of note

The 48-page inventory of 1899 lists a huge amount of furniture in the Drawing Room at this time, including six settees and 17 tables. The large cabinet was designed by H. W. Batley and made by Henry Ogden & Son, probably in

the 1870s. The table designed by Burges for Cardiff Castle has a central hole to accommodate a fully fruiting potted vine, allowing the freshest grapes to be picked by guests after a meal. The paintings include the remaining nucleus of the family's picture collection and portraits of the family.

The Conservatory

Built in 1963 to grow tender plants throughout the year and to allow winter gardening, the Conservatory was the last addition to the house. Over the years the building had deteriorated hugely and, in 2005, was replaced in cedar.

The Making of a Great Garden

Finding a formal Victorian garden much in decline, Sir John and Lady Heathcoat Amory's priority after the Second World War was to rescue and reinvigorate it. The result is an outstanding garden, whose plants represent one of the most varied and valuable botanical collections in the National Trust's care.

Opposite *Rosa banksiae* 'Lutea' on the outside of the house

Below The Terraces of the south front commanding views over Tiverton

The formal garden

'The idea has always been at Knightshayes to blend…. Gardening is really interfering with nature: it's man-made and you're putting the plants where you want them.'

Lady Heathcoat Amory, 1991

The planting on the house was introduced by Edward Kemp when Knightshayes was first built, the many nails attached to the walls evidence of his luxuriant creepers, trained to climb the walls.

The Terraces

The wrought-iron gates, designed in 2002, lead past the Conservatory to the Terraces on the south of the house. The view opens out across the park, which is separated from the grounds by the ha-ha, and beyond towards Tiverton and the Heathcoat factory. The view is framed by a Cedar of Lebanon, on the site of the earlier house's kitchen garden.

On the upper terrace a gravel path leads past the house's garden door to an herbaceous border where the east wing is set back. Planted in 1989 by Lady Heathcoat Amory, the yew hedges enclose trefoil-shaped beds containing mixed shrubs. The second terrace, now grassed over, contains a lead cistern bought in 1950. The stone eagles were installed in the 1920s and the urns after 1946. The path of the third terrace runs alongside a border planted in the soft colours so beloved by Lady Heathcoat Amory.

All that remains of the original 19th-century rose garden is the formal paving and traces of the former beds, still visible in the grass. The central dolphin fountain was added in the 1950s.

The Paved Garden

Beyond the house a gravel path on the top terrace leads towards a group of yew-hedged enclosures, clipped into crenellated forms of military precision. The Paved Garden, an area restored after the Second World War, is divided by a path with steps up to a lead cistern, dating from 1727 and bought from the Goldsmiths Company. On either side are stone benches, originally from the Bank of England and brought to

Knightshayes in the 1950s, together with two standard wisterias.

The flowerbeds between the paving stones are filled with alpines, small bulbs and other plants of softly coloured silver and grey foliage and yellow, pink and purple flowers. A terrace border alongside the gravel path is planted with small perennial alpine plants and bulbs. The original alpine plantings came from Nelly Britton of Bolham, a local alpine enthusiast, who supplied many of the plants.

Above **The Paved Garden**

Opposite top **The view over the Pool Garden**

Opposite right **The Fox and Hounds topiary reflects Sir Ian's great enthusiasm for hunting**

Staffing the garden

When Lady Heathcoat Amory came to live with Sir John after their marriage in 1937 there were 13 staff working in the garden, most of them in the Kitchen Garden. However, prior to Michael Hickson's arrival in 1963, only three gardeners remained. The chauffeur mowed the lawns around the house, whilst Sir John and Lady Heathcoat Amory tended the rest of their garden, which covered 12 acres at that time and finally grew to 30 acres. The garden and park are now maintained by six full-time gardeners and three trainees, supported by over 50 enthusiastic and knowledgeable volunteers.

The Fox and Hounds

South of the Pool Garden is a series of nine hounds chasing a fox around the top of the hedge. Cut in the 1920s for Sir Ian, it is a measure of his passion for countryside sports. At the far end of the lawn is a copy of the Borghese vase, the original of which was made in Athens in the 1st century AD as a garden ornament for the Romans and is now in the Louvre Museum in Paris. Below the Fox and Hounds hedge are a summerhouse and seats overlooking the South Garden.

The Pool Garden

On the other side of the yew hedge is the Pool Garden. Originally designed by Kemp in the 1870s as a bowling green, it was subsequently altered by Sir John and Lady Heathcoat Amory in 1957, and made into the garden seen today.

The round pond, in which golden orfe swim, is planted with different species of water lilies, including the red *Nymphaea* 'Escarboucle', white *N. gladstoniana* and yellow *Nymphaea* 'Moorei'. The overall formality is highlighted by the asymmetrically placed weeping silver pear tree, pruned to lean over the water, which, with the Victorian statue of a bather standing in a yew alcove, are reflected in its surface. A superb *Acer pseudoplatanus* 'Brilliantissimum' rises behind the encircling yew hedge.

The woodland garden

The Garden in the Wood

Following a pilot's tragic death at the end of the Second World War, when his P47 Thunderbolt plane hit the tops of several trees, Sir John and Lady Heathcoat Amory decided to begin a new garden after clearing away the broken trees.

Lady Heathcoat Amory was clear about her vision for this area – not a woodland garden but 'a garden in a wood'. Rising to the east beyond the formal gardens its creation was a huge task. During the 1950s and 1960s a piece of woodland about the size of a tennis court was added to the garden each year. Hundreds of trees were removed and, to the old Austrian and Scots pines, oaks and birches, which were retained, a wide range of plants was added, with advice from Sir Eric Savill and Norman Hadden. Sir John's passion was for acquiring the plants, whilst Lady Heathcoat Amory's love was for arranging them, with an eye to views, vistas, clearings and darker areas. To the end of her life, this remained her favourite part of the garden.

Above A path through the Garden in the Wood flanked by euphorbia, wood anemone, hellebore and massed azalea

A large pine grows in the centre of the first glade, with the adjacent planting formed mainly of camellias, magnolias, Japanese maples, rhododendrons and Kurume azaleas. Raised beds, formed with peat blocks which were inspired by a visit to Scotland by Sir John and Lady Heathcoat Amory, are ideal for small plants and bulbs. Planting to the east includes ericaceous shrubs as well as tree peonies, and rambling roses climb through the trees.

The garden now covers nearly 10 acres, with the old church path, which used to lead straight to Chevithorne church where the family had its own reserved pew, passing through the middle. It is surrounded with shrubs, underplanted with woodland herbaceous plants. Paths were an important component of the garden's design; on the opening of the garden to visitors Lady Heathcoat Amory declared, 'I do think paths have to have people on them – they're meant for it!'

The Glade

With the creation of the Garden in the Wood near completion the Heathcoat Amorys began the new challenge of developing the Glade, which Sir John saw as 'just the place for lilies'. Sheltered to the south by a mock orange hedge, planted at end of the 19th century, the focal point of the Glade is a large wooden seat.

The Flat Border to the west is planted with dwarf rhododendrons, camellias and creeping Canadian dogwood whilst, north of the hedge, a wide border is filled with plants in a purple, blue, yellow and green colour scheme.

The Island Bed is planted around a pittosporum. Creamy white and blue flowers fill the border behind a summerhouse known as the Cedar House, built in 1972, where part of the wing of the doomed aeroplane was found. At the east end of the Glade the hydrangeas, planted under the beech and pine, give a tunnel-like effect.

Right A springtime profusion of *Anemone nemerosa* and *Scilla messenaica* on the woodland floor

The South Garden

Playing a key part in framing the view towards Tiverton the sheltered three-acre South Garden has several large Turkey and other oaks, which appear to date from the involvement of John Veitch, the celebrated nurseryman and landscape gardener from Exeter. Records from 1794 show that Veitch had been 'lately employed at Knightshayes about the new house' but do not detail what this was. Although the first Sir John had demolished this 'new' house much of the planting was retained and used as a game covert. In 1937 it was converted to a nine-hole golf course with turf from the Tiverton golf course, a wedding present to Lady Heathcoat Amory from the tenants of the estate.

By 1954 it became clear that the large-leaved rhododendrons were not faring well in other parts of the garden; one of the many lessons learned the hard way, by trial and error. This area of the garden was more suitable and so the woodland was thinned, the ground prepared and the rhododendrons transplanted here, amongst the large exotic trees, including several varieties of southern beech. The glory of this garden, these islands of rhododendrons give the area a secluded feel and provide sensational colour and scent in the spring.

The area has a thickly planted perimeter, which provides shelter for the dogwoods and Japanese cherries, which add further colour to the garden. A 20th-century timber summerhouse stands next to the steps leading back to the Terraces. During its restoration in the early 1990s it was realised that the shields circling the inside of the summerhouse were, in fact, those from the Great Hall screen, which had been removed in 1914 and were restored to their rightful place when the screen was recreated in 1995.

Opposite A path through the Garden in the Wood leading to the English Woodland Walk

Above The summerhouse which at one time featured shields from the Great Hall screen

The English Woodland Walk

This peaceful area, a haven for wildlife, was created in 2000. The English Woodland Walk passes beneath the moss-covered branches of tall oaks and, in spring and summer, native plants such as anemone, narcissus and ferns cover the banks. This part of the garden has a natural, woodland feel and emphasises the beauty of nature's many shades of green. One of Lady Heathcoat Amory's favourite colours, she marvelled at the wide range of hues created by nature. Franklyn's Way, a broad pathway, is named after former Knightshayes deputy head gardener Franklyn Tancock.

The Arboretum

The Arboretum, lying to the north of the garden's central path, is an open relaxing space after the other more densely planted areas. Its vistas of mature ash, beech, oak and some conifers, offering views both through the glades and occasionally to the countryside beyond, are underplanted with ornamentals. A bank of mock orange borders the north side behind groups of sun-loving plants and a variety of grasses grows on the south-facing bank.

Michael's Wood

This wood, in the furthest south-east corner of the gardens, is named after Michael Hickson, who joined the staff as very young head gardener in 1963. Together Sir John, Lady Heathcoat Amory and he planned and developed the garden democratically. As she later explained, 'We used to go by a vote. If one had an idea, the other two had to agree to it.'

This part of the garden, developed in the early 1970s, is planted with a collection of Michael's favourite plants; under the trees is a wide range of woody plants, including bamboo and heaths, which provide contrasting foliage, shapes and colour all year round. Mahonias, Japanese maples and hydrangeas grow alongside swathes of hardy cyclamen, a particular favourite of Lady Heathcoat Amory's, under a fine stand of Douglas fir.

A world-class collection

Knightshayes' plant collection is one of the most comprehensive of all those cared for by the National Trust. The collection contains plants grown from seed gathered from the wild by some of the foremost plant collectors of the 20th century. Several of these have been named after Knightshayes itself, such as the pictured *Erythronium revolutum* 'Knightshayes Pink', which grows in Sir John's Wood.

Holly's Wood

This area of the garden finally reached its present size by the late 1960s. An informal planting of trees and shrubs, within the existing beech, oak and lime, stands to the north, around an open lawn area – an open-glade effect, contrasting with the intimate scale and dense planting elsewhere. The single larch remaining from the original planting, 'the Sentinel', stands alone on the lawn.

The wood was named after Herbert Hollinrake, a nurseryman and friend of the family from Ottery St Mary, who generously donated plants to the garden in the 1960s and '70s. A horseshoe-shaped planting effect on the north fringe consists of Chinese rhododendrons and some Asiatic magnolias, which go on to mingle with *Cercidiphyllum* and the white stems of a birch collection. Springtime brings a display of English and Mediterranean bluebells, followed by the fresh fronds of new ferns under the tree canopy.

Sir John's Wood

This was described by Sir John as 'a larch wood, the trunks making an impressive background with mysterious darkness beyond'. Many larches were felled during the Second World War, hauled out of the wood by horse and chains to be used for pit props in the coalmines. The severe storms of January 1990 caused the destruction of many more larches and, with them, the darkness noted by Sir John.

Some of these larch trees were retained and new species of larch were introduced to form a new canopy. All but one were felled in late 2012, this one left as it stands in glorious isolation in the middle of a lawn and has not suffered through disease and the loss of the shelter belt as the other larches had. The timber was used to create the new cricket pavilion in the parkland. The understorey of rare and wild collected plants still forms a year-round tapestry of shapes, sizes, colours and scents, just as Sir John intended.

Knightshayes' estate of gardens, pasture and woodland covers an area of over 260 acres

The Parkland

The wider parkland landscape has evolved from areas of lawn created in the late 18th and early 19th centuries and from areas of farmland, which were gradually taken into the park in the mid-19th century. Edward Kemp advised Sir John on the parkland planting. Old hedges were removed to open up vistas through the parkland, arable land was converted to pasture and metal railings and gates along the drive were introduced. These large metal-fenced grazing enclosures with scattered ornamental trees framing views over the surrounding landscape are still characteristic of Knightshayes' parkland.

To the east of the drive are significant groups of mature trees, including what is said to be the largest Turkey Oak in the country, and a mid-19th-century Wellingtonia survives from more extensive planting described in 1889 in the *Journal of Horticulture*.

The drive, running from Burges' Lodge to the Stables, is bordered by mown grass separated from grazed parkland by the estate fencing. Part of the estate is still owned by the Heathcoat Amory family, including the former Home Farm to the north of the house and parkland areas to the east and west of Trust property. Conservation schemes implemented on the estate include Natural England's Higher

Above Wildflowers and pasture in the parkland

Opposite The poolside path in dappled sunlight in the Azalea Dell, with yellow and pink azaleas

Level Stewardship Scheme, covering the tenanted farmland, and the Forestry Commission's Woodland Grants Scheme, which encompasses the woodland.

The cricket pitch in the park was provided by the Heathcoat Amorys for their employees at the factory and is the home of the Heathcoat Cricket Club. Its new clubhouse was built in 2012–13 on the site of the 1920s building, using traditional techniques and timber from the estate.

Woodland

Writing in *The Englishwoman's Garden* in 1983, Lady Heathcoat Amory described the woodland at that time: 'Regrettably, many of the fine old trees have now died, either from elm disease or as a consequence of the 1976 drought which was disastrous for the beech and birch trees. It had certainly never crossed our minds that mature trees could vanish almost overnight and we had not made a regular practice of planting up young forest trees. Quite rightly, tree planting is now recognised as a duty for the sake of future generations.'

This new planting has been undertaken by the National Trust since it acquired Knightshayes in 1972.

The Azalea Dell

In a valley west of the house and drive was Kemp's original 'American Garden', named after the many American plants it contained. The area was transformed by the Heathcoat Amorys with the planting of a selection of trees in the 1970s to create the Azalea Dell, one more major garden reclamation project.

Once containing an ambitious array of American and ericaceous plants, rockeries, ponds and waterfalls, today only the land form, pond and some old *Azalea mollis* and Ghent azaleas betray the origins of this garden, now planted with a willow collection, shrubs, small trees and drifts of spring daffodils.

The working estate

The Kitchen Garden

The walled garden, seen as an essential part of a Victorian country estate to provide food, flowers and even exotic fruit, was a clear statement of wealth, for both production and display. Covering an area of just over four acres on a south-facing slope it was probably designed by Burges in 1870, although none of his drawings have been found. Its stepped and coped walls, in local purple stone rubble with mellow shades of grey, include two corner towers with distinctive conical roofs. The internal layout of the garden, with its four main parts divided by lime mortar paths and further divisions of parallel grass paths bordered by half-standard fruit trees around a mulberry tree, was probably by Edward Kemp. The 19th-century head gardener's cottage, at the north-west corner of the garden, was occupied by Sir John and Lady Amory during the Second World War, to free up the main house for the armed forces.

In continuous production until the 1960s, and particularly essential during the two World Wars, the garden then fell into disrepair, was grassed over and the gates locked. The National Trust began a major programme of restoration in 2001, the garden opening in

The Douglas Fir Walk
Bordering the east end of the Kitchen Garden is the Douglas Fir Walk. The species was introduced into Britain from the Rocky Mountains in 1827 by David Douglas. This avenue of Douglas firs at Knightshayes, planted in the 1870s, is today one of the most important stands of these trees, including some of the largest, in the country.

Above Courgette 'Genovese' growing in the Kitchen Garden

Opposite A view over the Kitchen Garden in July

Right Produce from the Kitchen Garden for sale

Below A trugful of summer fruits fresh from the Kitchen Garden

2003. The layout of the old kitchen garden was recreated, retaining as many of the original features as possible, such as the axial yew-hedged paths, the mulberry trees at the *rond points* either side of the central dipping pond and the topiary at the south west end. One of the gates leading into the garden was designed in 2008 by Stanley Yeo, who worked on the estate for his entire life.

Growing organically
Today the garden is cultivated on organic principles, following the Victorian gardening approach of 'trying anything' and pushing the boundaries, with sustainability its main guiding principle. Heritage vegetables (including 102 varieties of heritage tomatoes) are grown amongst ornamental fruit, many of which are Victorian varieties. Produce from the garden is used in the restaurant and is sold to visitors to Knightshayes and at the Pannier Market in Tiverton.

The sections of the garden are divided into four rotational beds and four permanent beds,

the latter with fruit, vines, the heritage crops and the orchard, where chickens and geese run free. On the upper tier of the walled garden, hidden from sight, are the Mushroom House, Apple Store and a room used for drying flowers. The site of the 17 19th-century glasshouses to the north-west of the garden is now occupied by late 20th-century horticultural buildings.

The Stables

Near the Kitchen Garden, and about 200 metres from the house, the stable block is another Burges building. Built in 1871 and typical of his medieval style the building, with its asymmetric façade, red-painted dormer windows and dominant clocktower, is today surrounded on three sides by trees and partially covered in creepers. The stable block, following traditional designs, has four ranges built around a courtyard of granite setts.

It originally comprised looseboxes, a chaff house, a hayloft, a cleaning and harness room and a carriage house. In the late 19th century, the age before motor cars, Sir Ian, later 2nd Baronet, owned three carriages – a trap for everyday use, a brougham, with its enclosed body and a Victoria, an elegant carriage with a

The sticke tennis court

Situated near the Stables, this timber-clad building is still owned by the family and not accessible to visitors. Sticke tennis was a racquet sport invented in the late 19th century, combining aspects of real tennis, racquets and lawn tennis, and played with standard lawn tennis racquets and low-pressure balls. A popular recreation at many Victorian country houses it was, at the time, one of the few games played by both men and women. Knightshayes sticke tennis court is of great importance, being one of only three playable sticke courts in the world, the other two being at Hartham Park in Wiltshire and the Viceregal Lodge (formerly the residence of the British Viceroy of India and built in the 1880s) in Himachal Pradesh. Constructed of wood in 1907 and measuring about 78 by 27 feet, the tennis court was built for family members and their guests to play sticke tennis, with a maximum of 12 spectators, as stated by the notice on the outside of the building.

Above **The Stables seen from the Kitchen Garden in the 1960s**

Above right **The Heathcoat Amorys were passionate about hunting**

Right **The family used horse-drawn and later motor carriages**

fold-back cover, very popular with wealthy families. In 1904 Sir Ian bought his first car, an Arrol Johnson, in which he drove to Glasgow over a period of five days in 1906. Later he owned a Chrysler, followed by a Sunbeam and finally a series of Bentleys. Sir John, 3rd Baronet's first car was a Stutz, produced by the Stutz Motor Company, which was known as a supplier of fast, luxury cars to the wealthy. His brother Derick drove a more modest Austin Six.

Hunting was a passion for several generations of the Heathcoat Amory family and the Stables were important and busy right up until the 1940s when they were converted into accommodation for convalescing American airmen. After the War the building was converted to two flats, with stores for garden machinery. In 1988 it was restored and converted to provide the café, shop, lavatories and reception area for visitors.

At the Heart of Knightshayes

The Heathcoat Amorys played a significant role in the local community even before Knightshayes was built. The foundations laid by the family have been continued by the National Trust, keeping Knightshayes close to its community.

Ever since moving to Tiverton the Heathcoat Amory family have had strong links with the local community. John Heathcoat was praised by one of his workers in a letter of 1844, saying: 'We all have cause to pray for the life of Mr Heathcoat he is the best man that I ever knew in Tiverton for giving employment to the poor.' From John's election as Whig MP for Tiverton in 1832, later generations of the family continued to represent local people in Parliament and fulfil other community roles.

Playing host

The National Trust has sustained these links at Knightshayes, ensuring that the property still plays an important role in the community, with its support for local associations, such as the Heathcoat Trust, which assists students in the Tiverton and mid-Devon area, the Heathcoat Cricket Club and the Tiverton Spring Food and Drink Festival. As an educational resource it is perfectly equipped to support teachers with Victorian social history, firmly placed on the curriculum, and acts as an outdoor classroom for students of horticulture. Local groups, such as art and historical societies, also make good use of the property.

Above Knightshayes offers many educational opportunities

Opposite Knightshayes has always been at the heart of its community

Right A Christmas carol service rounds off the year's events at Knightshayes

Below A tea dance in the Great Hall

Joining forces

Knightshayes was used by the army during both World Wars, in the First as a Red Cross Hospital, and in the Second initially as a Casualty Clearing Station in the event of an invasion, but eventually as a rest home for US airmen.

During the First World War the entire ground floor of the house was equipped as a military hospital for 75 patients, with Lady Amory herself taking on a supervisory role. The family moved to the second floor of the house, where the bachelor rooms were situated, but very few structural alterations were required, with the exception of the Dressing Room, which became an operating theatre.

This page Life at Knightshayes during the Second World War

Roderick, brother of Sir Ian, 2nd Baronet who grew up at Knightshayes, remembers this time with fondness: 'As a boy of seven I found plenty to interest me in the hospital and spent a lot of my time playing billiards with the convalescent soldiers.' He also enjoyed driving the soldiers who could not walk into Tiverton in a donkey cart.

Knightshayes commandeered

In the Second World War, following the Dunkirk evacuation in 1940, injured British survivors convalesced at Knightshayes. Wearing blue serge suits they were known locally as the 'men in blue'. In 1942 the need was recognised for combat rest homes for airmen and so the American Red Cross was called in. Knightshayes became Ground Support Command Station 495, one of 14 British rest homes used by convalescing American airmen from the United States 8th Army Air Force, requisitioned as one of the so-called 'flak shacks'. The sticke tennis court near the stable block was furnished with hospital beds, as illustrated in the Screens Passage photo of 1940. During this time the family vacated the house for the head gardener's cottage near the Kitchen Garden and both Sir John and Lady Heathcoat Amory worked in the Tiverton factory, which turned to making parts for aeroplanes and parachutes.

Above The sticke tennis court furnished with hospital beds during the Second World War

Tragedy brings new beginnings

Very near the end of the Second World War a tragedy took place. It was the custom for departed occupants to return from their airfields in order to 'buzz' the house, which meant flying up the park almost at tree height, to applause and cheers from the Terraces. One fighter pilot dared too much and lost his life performing this stunt, his plane hitting the tops of several trees. The clearing away of the broken trees after the War was, more happily, the beginning of the Garden in the Wood.

The outlook for Knightshayes

Knightshayes – an extraordinary 19th-century house and a great 20th-century garden. It is a place where the significance of the past is preserved but always with an eye to a sustainable future.

Knightshayes is always changing. In 1991 Lady Heathcoat Amory said, 'I don't think a garden is the thing to keep.… It's either growing or dying, it's changing all the time. I don't think it's possible to try and keep it exactly as it used to be, nor do I think you'd want to.'

The same can be said of the whole property, with change bringing both challenges and opportunities. The Grade I listed status of the house and Grade II* Registered garden, the complex balance of conservation requirements of the property and the need to make it accessible to the public, and the limited funds available to maintain house, garden and estate, all represent challenges.

However, the continuity of vision for Knightshayes, begun by Sir John and now held in the National Trust's care, has given a firm and sustainable foundation for its future.